ANN WRIGHT

How to Love a Cat

Beginner's Guide to Raising and Loving a Cat

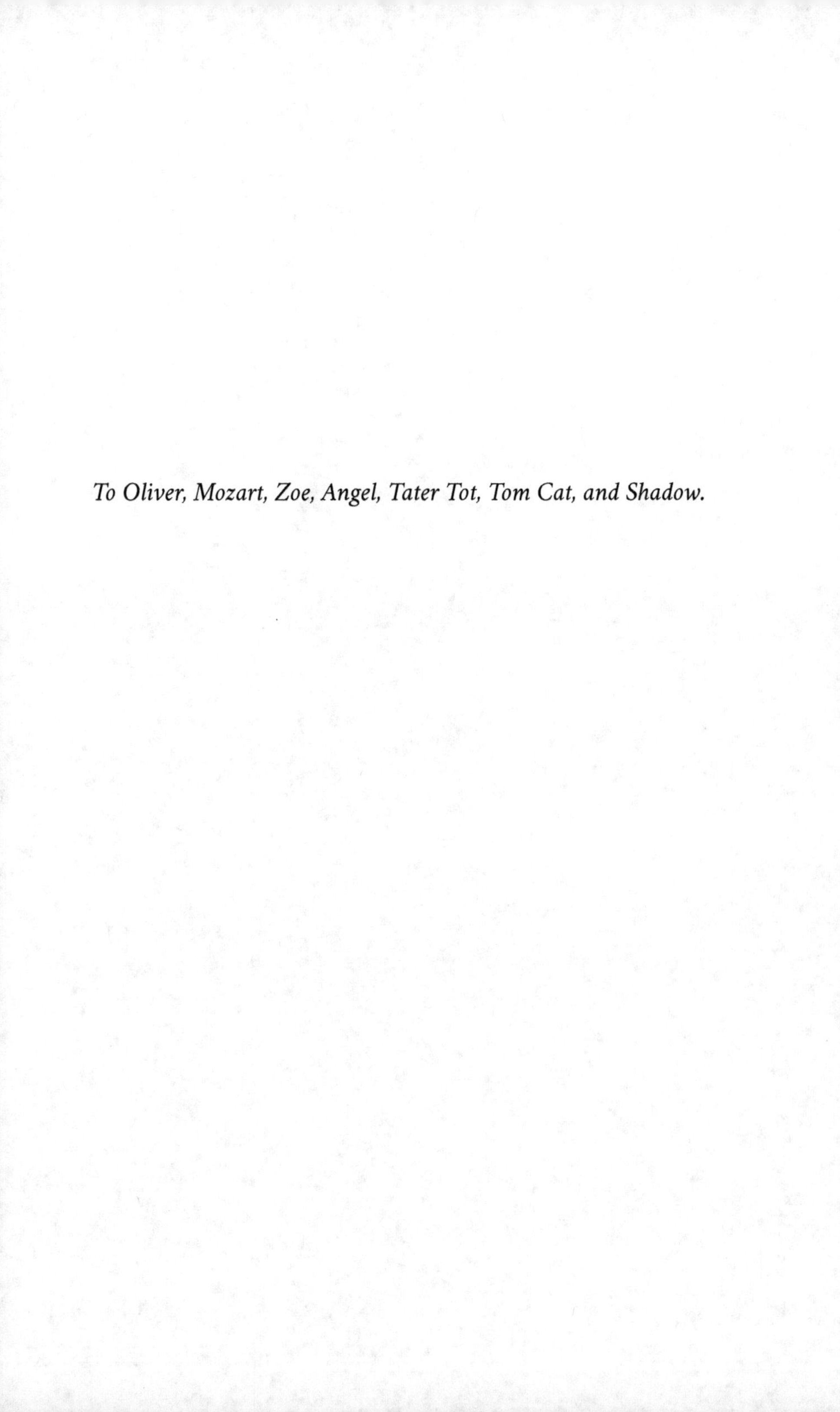

To Oliver, Mozart, Zoe, Angel, Tater Tot, Tom Cat, and Shadow.

Contents

1

Introduction

Welcome to *How to Love a Cat*. All the information that is in this book is information that I've been wanting to tell for a long time. Strangely enough I never thought to put this into a book. I was actually waiting for this conversation to organically come up and allow me an hour or two to dispense my knowledge uninterrupted. Most likely on some poor unsuspecting person who probably doesn't own a cat and never intends to, but instead was merely making an observation or comment. As you can guess that opportunity never presented itself and now my friends know never to bring up cats unless they want me to rant. So finally instead of waiting for a situation that would never happen I decided to write this all down for anyone who cares to listen. Hopefully this information finds itself in the hands of people curious to learn and I hope you find this helpful.

I've been an animal lover since birth I'm pretty sure. Over the years I've had all kinds of pets including hamsters, fish, dogs, and one mouse. But through it all cats were always a constant and eventually cats became my only pet of choice. My first cat was a boy tabby named Oliver, affectionately nicknamed Garfield for his striking resemblance, and Washing Machine as a running joke because of his loud purring ("who

1

left the washing machine on? Oh it's just Oliver"). He was a stray that was found by our mailbox when he was a few years old as was I at the time. He lived for 16 years and I loved him through all of them. I've had seven cats as of now and no not at the same time. Right now I only have one long haired tabby mix named Tom Cat, full name Tom Cat Tot. His brother's name was Tater Tot, no middle name. Tom and his brother were also strays. It also turned into a joke how many strays found their way to me. But I've loved having each and every one of them. And now I'm going to put everything I've learned and experienced in here for you. I hope you find this helpful.

I dedicate this book to all the cats in my life. Without them I would have no reason to write this book. I have decades of great memories with all of them and I hope you do as well with yours.

2

What to Expect

This book is a compilation of everything I've experienced as a cat lover for many years. I wrote this for people who have never owned a cat before or maybe have never even been around one before. If this isn't you no need to worry, the information in here is still helpful as I also talk about possible problems that may happen with your cat and possible solutions. So if you're a present cat owner in need of some advice or a previous owner with misgivings I hope you will gain some insight. So don't put down this book just yet.

Obviously this book is a small one. I could have made this longer and much much more in depth but I wanted this to be a more intimate book. I wanted this book to be a short read to get you on your way to owning a great cat. I wanted this to help people who might be on the fence or are merely curious. I don't want you to spend too much time in 'Research Land' where you might never return from. This book is going to provide the most vital and necessary information on how to live and interact with your cat. And hopefully stop any future misunderstandings you might have. So after you've read this you feel confident to go out and get your own cat with no fear and only love.

3

How to Choose Your Cat

If you haven't chosen a cat yet here are some things to keep in mind when looking. Just like every person is different, every cat is different. They all have different personalities, quirks, and baggage. While you're looking, take the time to just look and interact with each cat.

Some cats might be more affectionate or less affectionate. Some might be shy, some might be outgoing. Some might be loud, some might be quiet. Try to get to know the cat before choosing and don't assume the cat will change when you bring them home. And understand that whoever your cat is, you can't force your cat to be what it isn't. This is why it's important to choose a cat that clicks with you based on their behavior not on how they look or how old or young they are. Trying to force your cat to be something they aren't will only end up in an unhappy household. If you want a cuddler or social butterfly then don't choose a very shy cat that won't approach you when you meet them.

So for this reason my only advice for choosing a cat would be to go with your gut feeling. I would also recommend having everyone go and choose the cat together. Whether that's the whole family, a close friend, a roommate, or just yourself. This way all parties involved get to have a first time bonding experience with your soon to be cat. It can also prevent choosing a cat that might clash with the people you interact with.

4

How to Communicate With Your Cat

Interacting with a cat can seem difficult or confusing at first but once you learn, it's life changing. Think of it like learning a foreign language - but it takes much less time to learn. The biggest thing to start off with is you need to put your observation skills on full blast. Cats speak most of their language through body language. That's their natural language. When they're speaking with their mouth that is usually them trying to imitate our human language to communicate with you. So if they're willing to try for you, you need to try for them.

So first you want to observe your cat and then never stop because that is how they will communicate with you. First place to notice is their tail. When walking around if they're happy and content it will stand straight up. When their tail is down that doesn't mean they're sad it can mean a few things. When your cat first arrives in a new location as they explore their tail might be down and that's because they're cautious as they are in new unexplored territory. Of course it can also happen when they are scared. And when their tail is swishing or very flippant, sudden erratic flicks usually means they are about to hunt or they're annoyed. So unless you're playing with them that would be the time to back off what you're doing.

Ears are another good location to keep tabs on. If their ears are up then everything is good. When their ears flatten on their head that means they are either scared, anxious, nervous, or angry. The flatter their ears are to their head the more intense their feeling. This is another time to stop or remove whatever is causing this behavior and allow your cat to calm.

Another place to watch that's easy is their eyes. We all know how pupils work in general when interacting with light but cats also have behaviors attached to theirs. When cats get scared or feel threatened their eyes will get big and so will their pupils making their iris almost completely disappear. If you're a first time cat owner and you see this behavior I encourage you not to approach especially if your cat is reacting this way towards you.

When you bring a cat to a new environment they may need time to acclimate. This may include finding the first thing they can find and hiding underneath it. If this happens just let them be. They need to calm themselves first before going out and exploring the rest of the environment. If you try to remove them with an arm or hand or try moving the furniture your cat may get scared and resort to violence to protect themselves or just run under something else. This will just set you back in terms of trust with your cat because for them to love you and your place they first need to feel safe. It may be frustrating but the best you can do is let them hide and give them space and go about your business. You can always put a bowl of water and food close by if it seems they're going to be there for a while.

There is a time when cats will make noises in their own language and not just for the benefit of their human. When they feel threatened, angry, and scared they will make a disturbing meow growl. I would insert a clip of it but I can guarantee when you hear it you know your cat is telling either you or another animal to back off. The best thing to do is give them space and do not try to pet or pick them up even if their emotions are not directed at you. Patience is key. Especially in the beginning of your relationship when you're still trying to get to know each other.

5

Where and How to Pet Your Cat

Petting a cat is so fun and rewarding when your cat is super cute. But you have to keep in mind that your cat is a living being and not a plush toy. This means that sometimes you might want to pet your cat and your cat will say no and you have to respect that. Every cat is different and there are some exceptions to every rule but when you're a first time cat owner it's best to start off safe before you go exploring your cat's boundaries. Cats usually prefer soft petting and are not into rough pets, hair tousling, or being squeezed. If you have young kids it is especially important to teach them the appropriate way to pet them. Otherwise your cat might have an antagonistic relationship with them.

The safest places to pet your cat are their head and neck. You can do a full swipe pet from the top of their head to their neck. You could scratch under their chin or on their cheeks or rub the top of their head. These are the safest things to start with.

Next would be a full body pet from their head to their back but stop at their tail. It's best to only pet them in the same direction from head to back and not the other way around.

Some definite areas to avoid would be their bellies, their paws, and as

I said their tails. Their tails and their paws are very sensitive. Even light touches go a long way on these areas which is why many cats prefer not to be touched there.

A cat's belly I've found to be the trickiest. If you've ever had a dog or seen a dog you know they love belly rubs. So when a cat is being cute and has their belly exposed to you it might seem very hard to resist rubbing. It might even seem confusing why they do this if they don't want their belly rubbed. Cats do this to let you know that they trust you. They know you won't hurt them so they expose their most vulnerable part of themselves. Don't break that trust and pet their bellies. It might seem confusing and you might think they are baiting you but they're not. Feel free to pet their heads if you can't resist but know this is a sign of trust not an invitation.

6

How to Hold Your Cat

Holding your cat can be tricky to figure out. The best thing to do is observe your cat and take your cues from them. Some cats don't like being picked up at all. Some cats are more 'lap cats' preferring to sit on laps. And some cats are okay with being picked up but only for a short amount of time. If your cat is amenable to being picked up there are a few things to keep in mind. When holding them try not to hold on to their feet, just let them hang free.

I find the best way to hold a cat especially if the relationship is new is to have their front paws on your upper arm or shoulder and with your other arm cradle their legs against you without touching their feet.

If every time you try to hold your cat they immediately squirm and try to jump from your arms you might have a cat that doesn't like being picked up.

If you're still in the trying phase of feeling out if your cat likes to be picked up you can try mini holds. Where you go to pick up your cat but only lift them up part way. You can just lift their upper body off the floor but have their legs touch the ground. You can fully lift them from the ground but only a foot in the air and then immediately place them back down.

You can do this to gauge how your cat feels. In the beginning I wouldn't try picking them up as a surprise attack. I would pet them first so they know you're there and then go into the mini holds.Some might go limp and allow the hold, others might squirm or jump. Just take it slowly and know that there are cats that don't like being picked up.

But if your cat is responding well or seems to be coming around I have two basic ways to hold your cat.

First way to hold your cat is by standing in front of them and lifting them with your hands under their front paws, where their front legs meet their body. The other way to practice would be to start behind them and put one hand on their chest and the other hand on their belly and lift. Putting them in the same end position against your chest.

When to pick up your cat for the first time is completely up to you. With some cats being more outgoing than others I don't have an exact timeframe. I would just use your best judgment on when your cat is feeling comfortable around you.

7

Litter Boxes and Water Bowls

When you're prepping your home for a new cat there are things that you'll need to prepare. Some things are more necessary than others.

Litter boxes are essential and you'll want to have them already set up and ready to go in your home. How many litter boxes you'll need depends on how many cats you're getting or have already. You want to have the same number of litter boxes as you have cats plus one. So if you have one cat then you should get two litter boxes. If you have three cats then you should have four litter boxes and so on. The type of litter and the type of litter box is going to be subjective to your cat. Some cats are finicky and some won't care. This process is more trial and error on the cats preference. One thing I would definitely recommend is when introducing your cat to your home for the first time placing them next to the litter box first and foremost. This way they know where it is. If your cat is shy and is hiding and doesn't seem to be as sociable it will still know where to go to the bathroom.

When it comes to the number of water bowls I use the same method with litter boxes - have one for each cat plus one. Food bowls are mostly the same. If you have one cat then one food bowl is enough. If you have more than one cat I go back to the litter box method to avoid territorial issues which could happen.

8

Cat Accessories

There are a lot of things you can get for your cat to make them more comfortable or entertained. A lot of these things you don't need but can definitely make your cat happy and possibly help your cat. Cat beds are an easy to understand purchase. They have all kinds including some that come heated. I find these work really well if you have a cat that loves to lay on the floor a lot. A lot of the cats I've owned have been climbers and only liked to sleep on high but if you have a cat that likes to prowl low to the ground this could make them happy.

Cat trees are a nice vertical space for cats that like to climb but in a positive way. Putting a cat tree in a room most used by you and anyone else will help promote it. It's also nice because it promotes where you're okay with your cat jumping and climbing. Otherwise they may try to find somewhere else to climb like tables, counters, and cabinets. If you think your cat would benefit from the vertical space but a cat tree is too bulky or too expensive a less expensive version of this is floating shelves. This allows you to place as many as you would like and they take up less space.

A catio is also an idea if you have some outdoor space. If you're unfamiliar with this term it's just a cat patio. It gives your cat a feel of the outdoors but with all the safety. You can always buy one or make one if you're up for it. Sometimes just making a little fenced in space for them outside is a nice break for them from the indoors because many if not all cats really enjoy napping outdoors in the sun.

Another must have are scratching posts. These are essential if you don't want your cat tearing up all of your furniture. There are many types of scratching posts and you'll have to find the kind your cat is interested in first. In the beginning you can start with a variety of scratching posts. For protecting most furniture I'd recommend upright scratching posts placed next to them. There are also horizontal scratching posts made to be used while sitting on top of them which can be helpful if you're protecting carpet. Cat trees will usually come with scratching posts already implemented as a nice bonus.

9

Cat Toys

Playing with your cat can be really fun and also a great opportunity to see your cat being adorably aggressive. Every cat is different and each cat will take differently to different toys. This will be a trial and error period. Your cat might not even need an official toy. I've known cats to play with shoe laces, brown packaging paper, my fallen hair ties, and pens. No matter what toy you use it doesn't really matter as long as you play with your cat everyday for 10-15 minutes. It's important to get your cat active to burn off their energy. If not their energy can leak out in some undesirable behavior such as knocking things off tables, counters and shelves, and meowing in the middle of the night to say a few.

If you have to leave your cat alone there are ways to keep your cat occupied by themselves by using more creative toys. Treat puzzles are a great way to get your cat active and thinking. They can also come in handy if you need to slow down a fast eater, you can exchange the treats for their normal dry food. Treat puzzles are a way to get your cat focused and moving around using food as an incentive.

Another tool is having a cat tv. This can be a lot of things. The most common example that costs you nothing is a window. If you have a window you can use it to entertain your cat even while you're not there. If there is nothing exciting going on you can try to liven it up. If there isn't a view you might want to cut down some of your plant life if you can. Maybe add a bird feeder right outside to attract more commotion for your cat to watch.

If a window isn't working there are indoor ways to create a cat tv. There are fake mini fish tanks to get your cat stalking some prey. There are battery powered toys such as mice or other animals that will go running and so many more. The possibilities are endless.

10

How to Play With Your Cat

Playing with your cat can not only be fun for your cat but fun for you as well. Watching your cat get intense and focused or a butt wiggle jump can be very entertaining. But before the fun can begin there are a few tips to keep play time -play time. If you're a first time cat owner, playing with a cat is a new experience. Before you go on to play there are a few common mistakes people make when playing with cats that could cause problems down the line.

Biggest mistake I've seen when playing with a cat is playing with them like they are a dog. Cats and dogs are similar in many ways but they differ significantly in how they play. The biggest difference is rough housing. Dogs love it, humans love it (sometimes), cats can not handle it. And when I say cats can't handle it I'm actually referring to humans.

When playing with your cat do not use your hands or feet as a toy. Meaning don't rub them, poke them, or 'boop' them. And definitely don't do this using your hands or feet. Yes you've probably seen other people do this and yes you've probably seen videos of cats looking adorable. But what you also see or hear about are cats attacking their human's feet when they walk by, cats attacking their hands while trying to pet them and many more. This can sometimes look like your cat is

19

attacking you but most of the time it's actually your cat playing. Cats can't distinguish between playtime and not playtime. When they see their toy they're going to play and if you play with your cat using your hands or feet then that's what they will see as their toy.

It's just less cute when it involves your limbs. But that is the problem. When you rough house play with your cat using your hands or your feet you're teaching your cat that your hands and feet are toys. And cats would love nothing more than to play all day long (when they're not sleeping). So when cats think of your limbs as toys anytime they see your limbs whether they're moving or not your cat will start playing and those teeth and claws are no joke. So keep your hands for petting only for your own safety. I know they're cute and they're cuteness makes you want to squeeze, rub, and poke but resist.

If you're in bed and under the covers don't use your feet as a toy for your cat to jump on. Because in the middle of the night when you move your cat will jump on them. And keep in mind cats are nocturnal.

Some specific examples of rough housing that could turn wrong. Some people like to ruffle cat's hair or rub a cat's belly. When you do this a cat might try swiping at you, grabbing your hand and biting it, grabbing your hand to then use their back feet to kick and claw you. Some people may think it is cute when they're on their back with their paws in the air poised to strike. But again you are teaching them to associate your hands with play and don't think that they'll only play when you're ready for them.

You can say goodbye to picking them up because they might not trust your hands. Or once you have them in your arms they might start swiping and or biting.

It's also this misunderstanding that can cause frustration and anger towards your cat if you don't understand the reasoning behind their behavior. Because some cats genuinely don't like rough housing. If you're playing with them using your hands or feet and your cat's ears are down, they are not enjoying it. This can cause them not to play back but to actually attack because they think you are attacking them. And if you continue your cat may start seeing you as a threat. All of this can turn into an unhappy household without you noticing.

I don't want you to have a negative experience with your cat. And for that reason I share this information in hopes that it prevents misunderstandings and misgivings between you and your cat.

11

As Your Cat Gets Older

Observation is going to be key as your cat gets older. But over time you will get to know your cat so you more than anyone else will be able to tell when something's wrong. The vet will be your best friend. They are the best. They can always help give specific help with health problems you're having. Just make sure to document your observations of your cat so you know what to say to your vet and you don't forget anything.

Dry food is the go to for cats usually but as your cat gets older so do their teeth and stomach. This is where wet food can really come in handy. Wet food is a good thing to have in addition to the dry food to give your cat the option if they have teeth problems. Wet food comes in a variety of types. Some are more of a pate and some are more chunky and some are more like soup. To find the best type, talk to your vet for the best recommendations.

As your cat gets older your cat will have less energy. This doesn't mean that they no longer want to play or that they don't need to move around a bit. This is the time where you might need to get creative. One way to do that is using less active toys that still grip their attention and get them off their butt even if it's just to get from point A to point

B. Examples of such things are treat puzzles, cat TV, and a catio.

One of the big things you will need as your cat gets older are stairs. You'll want to place these around your home in places you want them to go but maybe they can't anymore. Some places I've had to place stairs are my couch, my bed, and their cat tree. You can't start using stairs too early so get them even if you're not sure. Your cat will use them if they feel it's necessary. Sometimes they might use the stairs to walk up because jumping up takes a lot of momentum but then jump down without the stairs. Your cat will use it when they're ready so have it on standby.

12

Conclusion

I hope the information in this book helps you in some way. I hope this has encouraged you to become a cat owner. And I hope that this book helps you have a great relationship with your cat. Over the span of time I've had cats I've seen and made many mistakes, including the ones you've read about above. I adore cats and truly think that they are amazing companions to have with you. I think understanding them through this book will help you so if you had any doubts or misgivings I hope they're all gone.

Hope this book was useful for you. If you liked it, let me know on Amazon by leaving a review.

13

Resources

Jackson Galaxy. (n.d.). *Behavioral Tips Archives*. Retrieved June 13, 2022, from https://www.jacksongalaxy.com/blog/tag/behavioral-tips/

C. (2022, April 25). *Cat Care 101: A Guide for New Cat Owners*. PetHelpful. Retrieved June 14, 2022, from https://pethelpful.com/cats/cat-care-101

Bingham, A. (2018, August 27). *5 Ear Signals Every Cat Owner Should Know*. iHeartCats.Com. Retrieved June 14, 2022, from https://iheartcats.com/5-ear-signals-every-cat-owner-should-know/

Parker, E. (2020, March 16). *A Guide To Petting Your Cat: Do's, Don't's, And Petting Zones*. Catological. Retrieved June 14, 2022, from https://www.catological.com/dos-donts-petting-cat/

www.ingramcontent.com/pod-product-compliance
Lightning Source LLC
Chambersburg PA
CBHW071505150726
48000CB00006B/2701